# AAT

## Management Accounting Techniques

### Pocket Notes

These Pocket Notes support study for the following AAT qualifications:

AAT Diploma in Accounting – Level 3

AAT Certificate in Bookkeeping – Level 3

AAT Diploma in Accounting at SCQF Level 6

## British library cataloguing-in-publication data

A catalogue record for this book is available from the British Library.

Published by:
Kaplan Publishing UK
Unit 2 The Business Centre
Molly Millars Lane
Wokingham
Berkshire
RG41 2QZ

ISBN 978-1-83996-603-3

© Kaplan Financial Limited, 2023

Printed and bound in Great Britain.

# CONTENTS

## Preface

These Pocket Notes contain the key points you need to know for the exam, presented in a unique visual way that makes revision easy and effective.

Written by experienced lecturers and authors, these Pocket Notes break down content into manageable chunks to maximise your concentration.

Quality and accuracy are of the utmost importance to us so if you spot an error in any of our products, please send an email to mykaplanreporting@kaplan.com with full details, or follow the link to the feedback form in MyKaplan.

Our Quality Co-ordinator will work with our technical team to verify the error and take action to ensure it is corrected in future editions.

# A guide to the assessment

## The assessment

MATS is the management accounting unit on the Diploma in Accounting qualification.

## Examination

Management Accounting Techniques is assessed by means of a computer based assessment. The CBA will last for 2 hours 30 minutes and consist of 6 tasks.

In any one assessment, students may not be assessed on all content, or on the full depth or breadth of a piece of content. The content assessed may change over time to ensure validity of assessment, but all assessment criteria will be tested over time.

## Learning outcomes & weighting

| | | |
|---|---|---|
| 1. | Understand the purpose and use of management accounting within organisations | 10% |
| 2. | Use techniques required for dealing with costs | 15% |
| 3. | Attribute costs according to organisational requirements | 20% |
| 4. | Investigate deviations from budget | 15% |
| 5. | Use spreadsheet techniques to provide management accounting information | 15% |
| 6. | Use management accounting techniques to support short-term decision making | 15% |
| 7. | Understand principles of cash management | 10% |
| Total | | 100% |

## Pass mark

To pass a unit assessment, students need to achieve a mark of 70% or more.

This unit contributes 30% of the total amount required for the Diploma in Accounting qualification.

# 1

## Management accounting

- Financial accounting and management accounting.
- The nature of cost accounting.
- Basic terms in cost accounting.

# Financial accounting and management accounting

### Definition

Financial accounts are an historical record of transactions which are presented in a standard format laid down by law. Such accounts are normally produced once or twice a year and are primarily used by external groups, e.g. shareholders.

### Definition

Management accounts can be produced in any format that is useful to an organisation. They tend to be produced more frequently than financial accounts, usually once a month. They contain information required to run a business.

Aims of management accounting – to assist management in the following areas

- Decision making
- Planning
- Co-ordinating
- Controlling
- Communicating
- Motivating

## Management Information

Management information needs to have the attributes of good information – it needs to be

ACCURATE:

**A**ccurate

**C**omplete

**C**ost-effective

**U**nderstandable

**R**elevant

**A**uthoritative

**T**imely

**E**asy to use

# The nature of cost accounting

**Cost accounting** is the process of calculating and recording the costs involved in the production and distribution of products and services.

Main reason for carrying out cost accounting: to calculate the cost of a product and therefore set the sales price of the item.

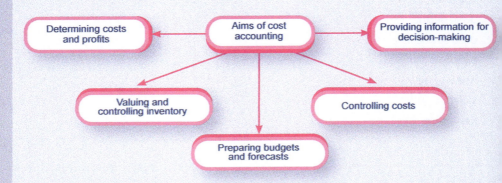

Determining costs and profits

Aims of cost accounting

Providing information for decision-making

Valuing and controlling inventory

Controlling costs

Preparing budgets and forecasts

# Basic terms in cost accounting

**Cost unit** refers to the item we are trying to find the cost of. This will normally be the item of a product that an organisation manufactures or a service that an organisation provides.

## Examples of cost units

| |
|---|
| Car manufacturer – car |
| Paint manufacturer – litre of paint |
| Accountancy firm – cost per chargeable hour |
| Hospital – cost per operation |

A **composite cost unit** is more appropriate if a service is a function of two variables.

## Examples of composite cost units

- Haulage company – tonne-mile
- Hospital – patient-days
- Public transport companies – passenger-miles

**Definition**

**A cost centre** is anywhere within an organisation where costs are incurred. A cost centre could therefore be a location, function or item of equipment.

**Key Point**

It is important to recognise that cost centre costs are necessary for control purposes, as well as for relating costs to cost units.

There are different types of centres determined by what the manager has control over:

- Cost centre
- Revenue centre
- Profit centre
- Investment centre

# Cost classification

- Cost cards.
- Cost classification.
- Element and nature.
- Function.
- Cost behaviour.
- High low method.

# Cost cards

A cost card is used to show the breakdown of the costs of producing output based on the classification of each cost.

|  | £ |
|---|---|
| **Direct costs** | |
| Direct materials | 250 |
| Direct labour | 120 |
| Direct expenses | 10 |
| **Prime cost** (Total of direct costs) | 380 |
| Variable production overheads | 15 |
| **Marginal production cost** (total of direct and variable costs) | 395 |
| Fixed production overheads | 35 |
| **Absorption cost** (total production cost) | 430 |
| Non-production cost | |
| (e.g. administration overhead; selling overhead) | 20 |
| **Total cost** | 450 |

# Cost classification

Cost can be classified as follows:

| Classification | Purpose |
|---|---|
| By element – materials, labour and expenses | Cost control |
| By function – production (cost of sales), and non-production (distribution costs, administrative expenses). | Financial accounts |
| By nature – direct and indirect | Cost accounts |
| By behaviour – fixed, variable, stepped fixed and semi-variable | Budgeting, decision making |

# Element and nature

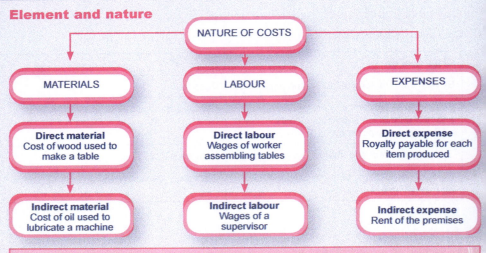

NATURE OF COSTS

**MATERIALS**

**LABOUR**

**EXPENSES**

**Direct material**
Cost of wood used to make a table

**Direct labour**
Wages of worker assembling tables

**Direct expense**
Royalty payable for each item produced

**Indirect material**
Cost of oil used to lubricate a machine

**Indirect labour**
Wages of a supervisor

**Indirect expense**
Rent of the premises

 Definition

Direct costs (prime costs) are costs that can be directly related to a cost unit.

Indirect costs (overheads) are costs that cannot be directly related to a cost unit.

## Function

### Production (operating costs)

Include production labour, materials, supervisor salaries and factory rent.

### Non production (non-operating costs)

Distribution – includes selling and distribution costs

Administrative costs – includes head office costs, IT support and HR support.

## Cost behaviour

A **variable cost** increases as the level of activity increases.

A **fixed cost** does not increase as the level of activity increases.

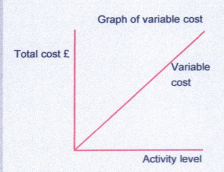

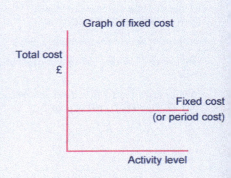

**Examples of variable costs:**

| |
|---|
| Direct materials |
| Direct labour paid using a piece-rate system |

**Examples of fixed costs:**

| |
|---|
| Business rates |
| Management salaries |

A **semi-variable cost** is one that contains both fixed and variable elements.

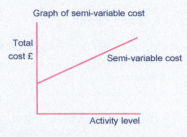

Graph of semi-variable cost

Semi-variable costs are also known as **semi-fixed costs** or **mixed costs**.

**Examples of semi-variable costs:**

| Electricity costs | – standing charge (fixed) + cost per Kwh used (variable) |
|---|---|
| Salesman's salary – basic (fixed) + bonus (variable) | |

A **stepped cost** is one that remains fixed over a certain range of activity, but increases if activity increases beyond that level.

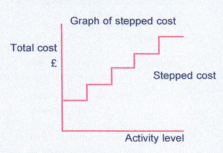

Graph of stepped cost

**Examples of stepped costs:**

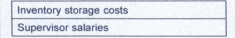

| Inventory storage costs |
|---|
| Supervisor salaries |

## High low method

If a semi-variable cost is incurred, it is often necessary to estimate the fixed and variable elements of the cost for the purposes of budgeting. The costs can be split using the high-low Method.

$$\text{Variable cost per unit (VC)} = \frac{\text{Change in total cost}}{\text{Change in level of production}}$$

Fixed cost = Total cost – (VC × units produced)

### Example

| Production units | Total cost £ | |
|---|---|---|
| 10,000 | 150,000 | |
| 12,000 | 175,000 | Solve using |
| 14,000 | 195,000 | High Low Method |
| 15,000 | 200,000 | |

**Solution**

1 Highest level of production =   15,000 units
(costing £200,000)
  Lowest level of production =   10,000 units
(costing £150,000)

2 Variable cost per unit

$$= \frac{\text{Change in total cost}}{\text{Change in level of production}}$$

$$= \frac{£200,000 - £150,000}{15,000 - 10,000} = \frac{£50,000}{5,000}$$

$$= £10$$

3 Substitute in lowest level of production
  Total cost for 10,000 units = £150,000
  = Variable costs of 10,000 units + Fixed costs
  Therefore fixed costs =
  £150,000 − (£10 x 10,000) = £50,000

KAPLAN PUBLISHIN

# Types of costing systems

- Marginal costing.
- Contribution and profit.
- Absorption costing.
- Marginal versus absorption costing.
- Job costing.
- Batch costing.
- Service costing.

# Marginal costing

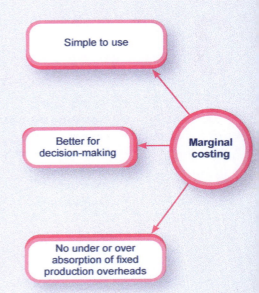

# Contribution and profit

**Contribution:** the difference between sales price of a unit and the variable costs of making and selling that unit.

**Profit:** the difference between total contribution and fixed costs.

| Example | | |
|---|---|---|
| The following data relate to product MWR for a period: | | |
| | | |
| Sales price | £10 | |
| Variable costs | £6 | |
| Units sold | 10,000 | |
| Fixed costs | £30,000 | |

| Contribution | |
|---|---|
| | £ |
| Sales price | 10 |
| Variable costs | (6) |
| | 4 |
| **Total contribution (TC)** | |
| TC = £4 × 10,000 = £40,000 | |

| Profit | | |
|---|---|---|
| Profit | = | Total contribution – Fixed costs |
| | = | £40,000 – £30,000 |
| | = | £10,000 |

**Remember!** There is a direct link between the total contribution and the number of items sold. However, there is no direct link between profit and the number of items sold.

# Absorption costing

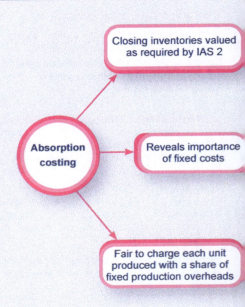

# Marginal versus absorption costing

The difference in inventory valuation between marginal and absorption costing gives rise to a difference in reported profits if there is a movement in inventory levels.

**CBA focus**

If you are not given opening inventory in a question, assume it equals 0 units.

---

**Fixed overhead per unit**

$$\frac{\text{Budgeted fixed overheads}}{\text{Budgeted production}}$$

$$\frac{£40,000}{10,000} = £4 \text{ per unit}$$

---

**Example – reported profits**

| | £ per unit |
|---|---|
| Sales price | 15 |
| Materials | 4 |
| Variable production costs | 2 |
| Budgeted fixed production overheads | £40,000 |
| Budgeted production | 10,000 units |
| Budgeted sales | 8,000 units |

---

**Contribution per unit**

| | £ |
|---|---|
| Sales price | 15 |
| Materials | (4) |
| Variable costs | (2) |
| Contribution | 9 |

---

**Profit per unit**

| | £ per unit |
|---|---|
| Sales price | 15 |
| Materials | (4) |
| Variable costs | (2) |
| Fixed overhead | (4) |
| Profit | 5 |

From the example on the previous page, we can calculate marginal and absorption costing profits:

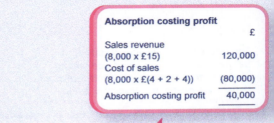

**Marginal costing profit**

| | £ |
|---|---|
| Sales revenue (8,000 x £15) | 120,000 |
| Cost of sales (8,000 x £(4 + 2)) | (48,000) |
| Contribution | 72,000 |
| Fixed overheads | (40,000) |
| Marginal costing profit | 32,000 |

**Absorption costing profit**

| | £ |
|---|---|
| Sales revenue (8,000 x £15) | 120,000 |
| Cost of sales (8,000 x £(4 + 2 + 4)) | (80,000) |
| Absorption costing profit | 40,000 |

Difference = £8,000

**Absorption costing**
Only (8,000 x £4) fixed overhead is written off against profit.
Each unit of closing inventory holds £4 fixed production overheads.

2,000 units of closing inventory hold 2,000 x £4 = £8,000 of fixed production overheads

## Layout of statement of profit or loss – marginal costing

| | £000 | £000 |
|---|---|---|
| Revenue (12,500 x £100) | | 1,250 |
| Cost of sales | | |
| (at marginal cost, £40) | | (500) |
| Contribution | | 750 |
| Less: Fixed production costs | 400 | |
| Fixed non-production costs | 150 | |
| | | (550) |
| Profit for the period | | 200 |

Fixed production overheads deducted in total from contribution.

## Layout of statement of profit or loss – absorption costing

| | £000 |
|---|---|
| Revenue | 1,250 |
| Cost of sales (at absorption cost, £72) | (900) |
| Gross profit | 350 |
| Less: Fixed non-production costs | (150) |
| Profit for the period | 200 |

Fixed production overheads are absorbed into cost of sales.

| Cost of sales per unit | £ |
|---|---|
| Marginal cost | 40 |
| Fixed cost £400,000/12,500 | 32 |
| | 72 |

## Job costing

**Definition**

**Job costing**: the costing system used for a business where production is made up of individual, different, large jobs.

### Businesses that use job costing

- Construction companies
- Aeroplane manufacturers
- Vehicle repairers.

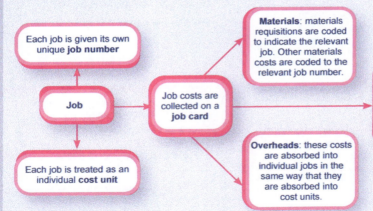

Each job is given its own unique **job number**

**Job**

Each job is treated as an individual **cost unit**

Job costs are collected on a **job card**

**Materials**: materials requisitions are coded to indicate the relevant job. Other materials costs are coded to the relevant job number.

**Labour**: employees working on individual jobs keep job time records and the cost of each employee for each job is recorded on the job card.

**Overheads**: these costs are absorbed into individual jobs in the same way that they are absorbed into cost units.

# Batch costing

**Batch costing:** the costing system used for a business where production is made up of different product batches of identical units.

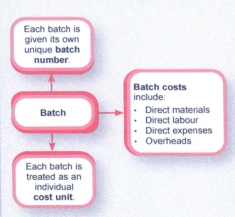

Each batch is given its own unique **batch number**.

**Batch**

**Batch costs** include:
- Direct materials
- Direct labour
- Direct expenses
- Overheads

Each batch is treated as an individual **cost unit**.

## Example

### Batch costing

GA Ltd is a paint manufacturer. 1,000 litres of 'polar white' matt vinyl paint are produced. The production run costs are as follows:

|  | £ |
|---|---|
| Materials | 1,600 |
| Labour (15 hours at £10 per hour) | 150 |

Overheads are absorbed at a rate of £16 per direct labour hour.

| Total batch cost | £ |
|---|---|
| Materials | 1,600 |
| Labour | 150 |
| Overheads (15 hours @ £16) | 240 |
| Total batch cost | 1,990 |

**Cost per unit for batch**

$$\text{Cost per unit} = \frac{\text{Total batch cost}}{\text{Number of units}} = \frac{£1,990}{1,000 \text{ litres}}$$

$$= £1.99 \text{ per litre}$$

## Service costing

Definition

Service costing is a form of **continuous operation costing**.

The output from a service industry differs from manufacturing for the following four reasons:

- **Intangibility** – the output is in the form of 'performance' rather than tangible or touchable goods or products.
- **Heterogeneity** – the nature and standard of the service will be variable due to the high human input.
- **Simultaneous production and consumption** – the service that you require cannot be inspected in advance of receiving it.
- **Perishability** – the services that you require cannot be stored.

# Materials

- Materials control cycle.
- Materials documentation.
- Cost of holding inventory.
- Holding costs.
- Systems of inventory control.
- Inventory control levels.
- The stores record card.
- Costing issues of raw materials.
- Equivalent units and work in progress.
- Integrated bookkeeping – materials.

## Materials control cycle

**Functions of stores department**

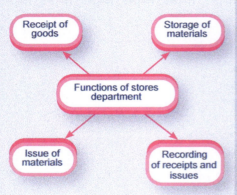

### Control of purchasing

It is necessary to ensure:

- only necessary items purchased
- orders placed with most appropriate supplier
- goods received match goods ordered
- correct price paid for goods.

# Materials documentation

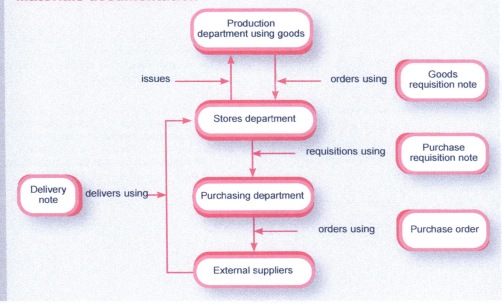

# Cost of holding inventory

Functions of inventory

### Inventory control

**Definition**

Inventory **control**: the method of ensuring that the right quantity of the right quality of the relevant inventory is available at the right time and in the right place.

**CBA focus**

There are a number of formulae associated with calculating inventory control levels – they are not provided in your assessment and so it is important that you learn them by heart.

# Holding costs

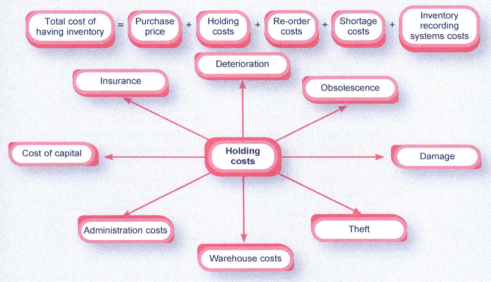

## Systems of inventory control

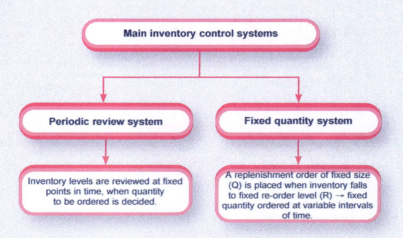

Main inventory control systems

Periodic review system

Fixed quantity system

Inventory levels are reviewed at fixed points in time, when quantity to be ordered is decided.

A replenishment order of fixed size (Q) is placed when inventory falls to fixed re-order level (R) → fixed quantity ordered at variable intervals of time.

# Inventory control levels

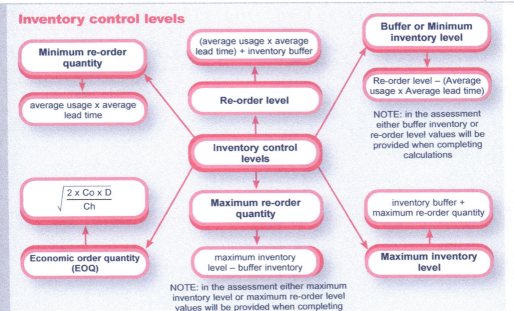

**Minimum re-order quantity**

average usage x average lead time

(average usage x average lead time) + inventory buffer

**Re-order level**

**Buffer or Minimum inventory level**

Re-order level – (Average usage x Average lead time)

NOTE: in the assessment either buffer inventory or re-order level values will be provided when completing calculations

**Inventory control levels**

$$\sqrt{\frac{2 \times Co \times D}{Ch}}$$

**Economic order quantity (EOQ)**

**Maximum re-order quantity**

maximum inventory level – buffer inventory

inventory buffer + maximum re-order quantity

**Maximum inventory level**

NOTE: in the assessment either maximum inventory level or maximum re-order level values will be provided when completing calculations

# The stores record card

**Definition**

Stores ledger account: deals with the accounting of materials (price and quantity) and is maintained by the accounting unit. Physical inventory shown on these accounts is reconciled with the bin card.

**Key Point**

When materials are received by stores department, they are checked to ensure correct quantity delivered. The details are then entered onto the stores record card (bin card) which may not have a price column.

| Typical stores record card | | | | | | | | |
|---|---|---|---|---|---|---|---|---|
| Material description : | | | Component X | | | | | |
| Code | | : | X100 | | | | | |
| Date | Receipts | | | Issues | | | Balance | | |
| | Quantity | Unit price £ | Total £ | Quantity | Unit price £ | Total £ | Quantity | Unit price £ | Total £ |
| | | | | | | | | | |

# Costing issues of raw materials

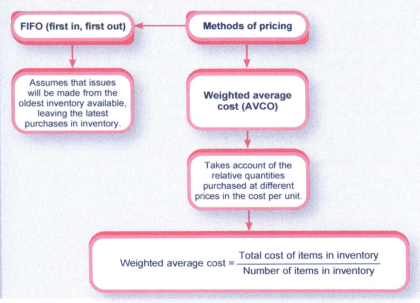

FIFO (first in, first out)

Methods of pricing

Assumes that issues will be made from the oldest inventory available, leaving the latest purchases in inventory.

Weighted average cost (AVCO)

Takes account of the relative quantities purchased at different prices in the cost per unit.

$$\text{Weighted average cost} = \frac{\text{Total cost of items in inventory}}{\text{Number of items in inventory}}$$

# Equivalent units and work in progress

**Equivalent units (EUs)**

Equivalent units concept

↓

Basis for splitting costs over complete and incomplete units.

↓

**Example – EUs**

1,000 units are 50% complete at the end of a period.

EUs = 1,000 × 50% = 500 EUs

Therefore, 1,000 units 50% complete are the same as 500 fully completed units.

## Cost per equivalent unit

- Calculated as: $\dfrac{\text{Total cost}}{\text{Number of EUs produced}}$

## Summary

- Calculate total EUs.
- Calculate total costs.
- Calculate cost per EU.
- Value the completed output and closing WIP.

## Example

### EUs and work in progress

In period 1 the following production occurred:
- Started and finished units = 800
- CWIP = 200 units each 35% complete

Costs in period 1 were £11,832.

**(1) Equivalent units**

**Units started and finished**
800 units x 100% = 800 units

**Closing WIP**
200 units x 35% = 70 units

**Total EUs**
800 + 70 = 870 units

**(2) Cost per EU** = $\dfrac{\text{Total cost}}{\text{Number of EUs produced}}$

= $\dfrac{£11,832}{870 \text{ units}}$ = £13.60

**(3) Valuation of outputs**

Completed units £13.60 per EU x 800 EU = £10,880

Closing WIP £13.60 per EU x 70 EU = £952

Total £11,832

# Integrated bookkeeping – materials

## Materials cost account

| | £ | | £ |
|---|---|---|---|
| Opening balance (1) | | Issues to production (4) | |
| Purchases (2) | | Returns to suppliers (5) | |
| Returns to stores (3) | | Production overheads (6) | |
| | | Statement of profit or loss (7) | |
| | | Closing balance (8) | |

(1) The opening balance of materials held in stores at the beginning of a period is shown as a debit in the material cost account.

(2) Materials purchased on credit are debited to the material cost account. Materials purchased for cash would also be a debit.

(3) Materials returned to stores cause inventory to increase and so are debited to the material inventory account.

(4) Direct materials used in production are transferred to the production account, which is also known as the Work-In-Progress. The is recorded by crediting the material inventory account.

(5) Materials returned to suppliers cause inventory levels to fall and are therefore 'credited out' of the materials cost account.

(6) Indirect materials are not a direct cost of manufacture and are treated as overheads. They are therefore transferred to the production overhead account by way of a credit to the materials cost account.

(7) Any material write-offs are 'credited out' of the material cost account and transferred to the statement of profit or loss where they are written off.

(8) The balancing figure on the materials cost account is the closing balance of material inventory at the end of a period. It is also the opening balance at the beginning of the next period.

# 5

## Labour

- Employee records.
- Remuneration systems.
- Direct and indirect labour costs.
- Overtime premium.
- Integrated bookkeeping – labour.

## Employee records

**Periods of absence** may include:

- Holidays
- Sickness
- Jury service
- Training courses
- Compassionate leave

**Personnel record details**

- Holiday allowance
- Name, address, date of birth
- Marital status, next of kin
- Bank details
- National insurance number
- Employee number/ clock number/ job title/department
- Employment history
- Date of joining/leaving
- Rate of pay/ salary details
- Educational and professional qualifications

**Attendance records** show hours worked by employees and are recorded on:

- Clock cards
- Timesheet

# Remuneration systems

REMUNERATION SYSTEMS

**Annual salaries** tend to be paid to managers and non-production staff

Gross pay (per month)

$$= \frac{\text{Annual salary}}{12}$$

**Hourly rates of pay and overtime payments**

Mainly apply to production and manual workers.

- Paid for every hour worked.
- Standard hours per week.
- Hours worked in excess of standard = Overtime hours.
- Overtime pay = Basic pay + Overtime premium.

**Piecework payments** are made when a fixed constant amount is paid per unit of output.

Disadvantages of this system include no security of income and being penalised for low levels of output which occur for reasons beyond an employee's control (e.g. machine breakdown). To overcome these disadvantages, the straight piecework rate is often accompanied by a **guaranteed minimum payment**.

# Direct and indirect labour costs

| Direct labour costs | Indirect labour costs |
|---|---|

**Direct labour costs**

↓

Production workers' wages

↓

Overtime premium when overtime worked at the specific instruction of a customer

**Indirect labour costs**

↓

Managers' and supervisors' salaries

Overtime premium when overtime worked due to general pressure of work.

Holiday pay

Training time

Controllable idle time

**Definition**

**Idle time:** non-productive hours that are paid for.

**Key Point**

The distinction between direct and indirect labour costs is a very important one.

# Overtime premium

## Definition

**Overtime premium** is the extra element of payment over and above the basic hourly rate for additional hours worked.

## Example

Court works a standard week of 40 hours at an hourly rate of £8.20 per hour. Overtime is paid at time and a half.

Last week Court worked 45 hours.

| Gross pay | |
|---|---|
| Basic pay = 40 x £8.20 = | £328.00 |
| Overtime = 5 x (£8.20 x 1.5) = | £61.50 |
| Gross pay | £389.50 |

### Overtime payment

Overtime hours = 45 – 40 = 5 hours

Overtime rate per hour = £8.20 x 1.5 = £12.30

Overtime payment = 5 hours x £12.30 = £61.50

### Overtime premium

Overtime premium is the amount paid over the basic hourly rate for the overtime hours

Overtime premium
per hour = 0.5 x £8.20 = £4.10

Overtime hours = 5

Overtime premium = 5 hours x £4.10 = £20.50

# Integrated bookkeeping – labour

**Labour cost account**

| | £ | | £ |
|---|---|---|---|
| Bank (1) | 80 | Production (2) | 60 |
| | | Production Overheads (3) | 20 |
| | 80 | | 80 |

(1) Labour costs incurred are paid out of the bank before they are analysed further in the labour account.

(2) The majority of the labour costs incurred by a manufacturing organisation are in respect of direct labour costs. Direct labour costs are directly involved in production and are transferred out of the labour account via a credit entry to the production account. The production account can also be referred to as Work in Progress (WIP).

(3) Indirect labour costs include indirect labour (costs of indirect labour workers), overtime premium (unless overtime is worked at the specific request of a customer), shift premium, sick pay and idle time. All of these indirect labour costs are collected in the production overheads account. They are transferred there via a credit entry out of the labour account and then debited in the production overheads account.

# Overheads

- Direct and indirect expenses.
- Allocation and apportionment of overheads.
- Bases of apportionment.
- Reapportionment.
- Methods of reapportionment.
- Absorption of overheads.
- Under/over absorption of overheads.
- Integrated bookkeeping – overheads.
- Activity Based Costing.

## Direct and indirect expenses

### Definition

All of the costs incurred by an organisation which are not materials or labour are known as **expenses**.

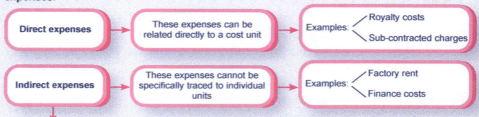

**Direct expenses** → These expenses can be related directly to a cost unit → Examples: Royalty costs / Sub-contracted charges

**Indirect expenses** → These expenses cannot be specifically traced to individual units → Examples: Factory rent / Finance costs

Also known as **overheads**

- **Production overheads** may be accounted for as part of cost of sales (factory rent, insurance, light and heat costs). This chapter focuses on production overheads and relating these costs to products.
- **Non-production overheads** may be accounted for below the gross profit line (administrative costs, selling and distribution costs).
- NOTE: In the real world the term "expenses" could include both direct and indirect components. In the exam, however, expenses are always treated simply as 'overheads' with no separation into direct and indirect elements.

# Allocation and apportionment of overheads

Definition

**Apportionment:** the splitting of shared overhead costs between relevant cost centres using an appropriate basis.

**Definition**

**Allocation:** charging the whole of an overhead cost to the specific cost centre that incurred it.

**Key Point**

Overheads may relate to several cost centres – for example, rent, rates and heating costs. Overheads which relate to several cost centres are shared out or **apportioned** between the relevant cost centres on the most appropriate basis.

**Key Point**

Overheads arise solely in a particular cost centre. The salary of a supervisor working exclusively in the assembly cost centre would, for example, be treated as an overhead and would be **allocated** to the assembly cost centre.

# Bases of apportionment

| Type of cost | Basis of apportionment |
|---|---|
| Maintenance | Number of hours worked/ machine time |
| Insurance of machinery | Carrying amount of machinery |
| Rent and rates | Floor space occupied $(m^2)$ |
| Lighting and heating | Volume occupied $(m^3)$ |

## Arbitrary nature of overhead apportionment

Overhead costs apportioned to different cost centres are simply the result of using a particular basis to share out the overall overheads of a business. If different bases had been chosen then the amounts apportioned to different cost centres would have been different, i.e. the overhead costs are shared out on an arbitrary basis.

## Example

**Bases of apportionment**

SB Ltd has two production departments (Assembly and Finishing) and two service departments (Maintenance and Canteen). The following costs are expected to be incurred.

| | £ | | |
|---|---|---|---|
| Indirect materials | 20,000 | → | Basis of apportionment = Direct allocation |
| Rent | 15,000 | → | Basis of apportionment = Area (m$^2$) |
| Electricity | 10,000 | → | Basis of apportionment = Kw hours consumed |
| Machine depreciation | 5,000 | → | Basis of apportionment = Machine value |
| Building depreciation | 10,000 | → | Basis of apportionment = Area (m$^2$) |
| Indirect labour | 55,000 | → | Basis of apportionment = Number of staff |

The following information is available:

| | Assembly | Finishing | Maintenance | Canteen |
|---|---|---|---|---|
| Area (m$^2$) | 1,000 | 2,000 | 500 | 500 |
| Kw hours consumed | 1,000 | 4,000 | Nil | 5,000 |
| Machine value | £45,000 | £35,000 | £11,000 | £9,000 |
| Number of staff | 20 | 30 | 10 | – |
| Indirect materials consumed | £7,000 | £8,000 | £3,000 | £2,000 |

The information given in this example can be used to calculate the overheads apportioned to the different cost centres. The ways in which this can be done are shown in the next example.

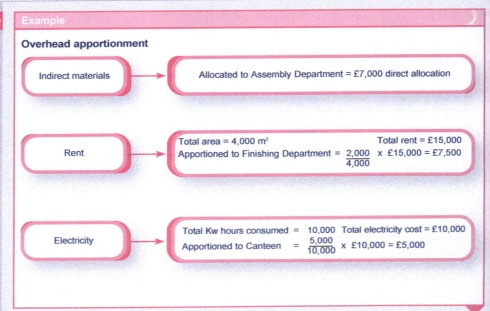

**Example**

**Overhead apportionment**

Indirect materials → Allocated to Assembly Department = £7,000 direct allocation

Rent → Total area = 4,000 m² | Total rent = £15,000
Apportioned to Finishing Department = $\frac{2,000}{4,000}$ × £15,000 = £7,500

Electricity → Total Kw hours consumed = 10,000 | Total electricity cost = £10,000
Apportioned to Canteen = $\frac{5,000}{10,000}$ × £10,000 = £5,000

## Example

### Overhead apportionment (continued)

**Machine depreciation**

Total machine value = £100,000     Total depreciation = £5,000

Apportioned to Maintenance $= \frac{11,000}{100,000} \times £5,000 = £550$

**Building depreciation**

Total area = 4,000 m² Total depreciation = £10,000

Apportioned to Assembly Department $= \frac{1,000}{4,000} \times £10,000 = £2,500$

**Indirect labour**

Total number of staff = 60     Total indirect labour = £55,000

Apportioned to finishing Dept $= \frac{30}{60} \times £55,000 = £27,500$

# Reapportionment

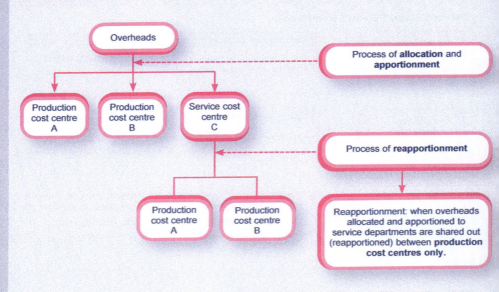

Overheads

Process of **allocation** and **apportionment**

Production cost centre A

Production cost centre B

Service cost centre C

Process of **reapportionment**

Production cost centre A

Production cost centre B

Reapportionment: when overheads allocated and apportioned to service departments are shared out (reapportioned) between **production cost centres only.**

# Methods of reapportionment

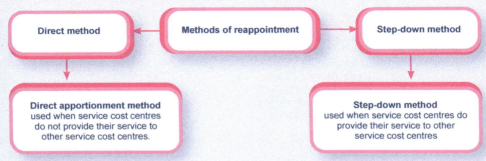

**Aims of reapportionment**

The reasons for reapportioning service department overheads is so that all costs are identified with a production cost centre and we can then work out the cost of the units produced by each production cost centre.

It is likely that the exam-based assessment you will be facing will require you to carry out a series of overhead allocations and apportionments.

# Absorption of overheads

## Absorption rate bases

Various overhead absorption rates exist and the most suitable one should be selected. The use of an absorption rate per unit is for one-product businesses but the following bases may be more appropriate for a multi-product business:

🔑 **Key Point**

Having collected all overheads in the production cost centres via overhead allocation, apportionment and reapportionment, the total overhead must be charged to the output of production cost centres. The charging of overhead costs to cost units is called **overhead absorption**.

- Absorption rate per direct labour hour
- Absorption rate per direct machine hour.

Direct labour hour rates are commonly used in labour-intensive production whereas direct machine hour rates are commonly used in machine-intensive production.

```
Calculated at the
start of a period
                          Overhead              Budgeted overheads
                          absorption rate   =   ──────────────────────
                                                Budgeted activity levels
Based on budgets
(estimates)
```

**g**

### Overhead absorption rates

Martin Ltd estimates that the total factory costs for the coming year will be as follows:

|  | £ |
|---|---|
| Direct materials | 40,000 |
| Direct wages | 60,000 |
| Prime cost | 100,000 |
| Factory overhead | 30,000 |
| Total factory cost | 130,000 |

The factory will produce 10,000 units of a variety of different products.

It is anticipated that during the year there will be 30,000 direct labour hours worked and 15,000 machine hours.

**Rate per unit**

$$= \frac{\text{Budgeted overheads}}{\text{Budgeted production}}$$

$$= \frac{£30,000}{10,000 \text{ units}} = £3 \text{ per unit}$$

**Rate per direct labour hour**

$$= \frac{\text{Budgeted overheads}}{\text{Budgeted direct labour hours}}$$

$$= \frac{£30,000}{30,000 \text{ hours}} = £1 \text{ per labour hour}$$

**Rate per machine hour**

$$= \frac{\text{Budgeted overheads}}{\text{Budgeted machine hours}}$$

$$= \frac{£30,000}{15,000 \text{ hours}} = £2 \text{ per machine hour}$$

# Under/over absorption of overheads

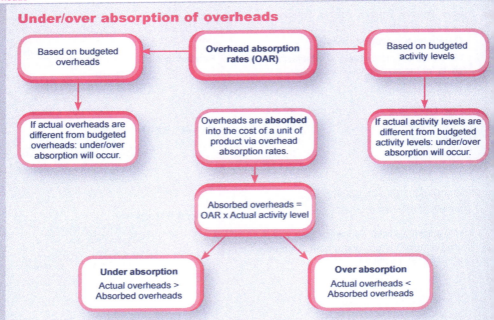

Overhead absorption rates (OAR)

Based on budgeted overheads

If actual overheads are different from budgeted overheads: under/over absorption will occur.

Based on budgeted activity levels

If actual activity levels are different from budgeted activity levels: under/over absorption will occur.

Overheads are **absorbed** into the cost of a unit of product via overhead absorption rates.

Absorbed overheads = OAR x Actual activity level

**Under absorption**

Actual overheads > Absorbed overheads

**Over absorption**

Actual overheads < Absorbed overheads

## Example

### Under/over absorption

A company has a single production department. Its budgeted production overheads for 20X4 were £200,000 and its budgeted volume of production was 50,000 direct labour hours. It has decided to absorb production overheads into product costs on a direct labour hour basis.

During 20X4, actual production overhead expenditure was £195,000.

Calculate the under or over absorption when:

(a) 54,000 direct labour hours are worked.

(b) 46,000 direct labour hours were worked.

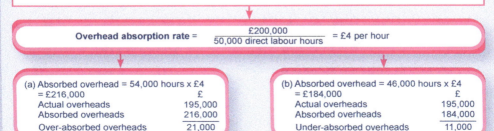

$$\text{Overhead absorption rate} = \frac{£200,000}{50,000 \text{ direct labour hours}} = £4 \text{ per hour}$$

| (a) Absorbed overhead = 54,000 hours x £4 | |
|---|---|
| = £216,000 | £ |
| Actual overheads | 195,000 |
| Absorbed overheads | 216,000 |
| Over-absorbed overheads | 21,000 |

| (b) Absorbed overhead = 46,000 hours x £4 | |
|---|---|
| = £184,000 | £ |
| Actual overheads | 195,000 |
| Absorbed overheads | 184,000 |
| Under-absorbed overheads | 11,000 |

# Integrated bookkeeping – overheads

## Production Overheads

| | £ | | £ |
|---|---|---|---|
| Actual Overhead cost (1) | | Absorbed overheads (2) | |
| Over-absorbed (3) | | Under-absorbed (4) | |
| | ___ | | ___ |
| | ___ | | ___ |

(1) The actual cost of all the indirect costs are recorded as a debit in the production overheads account. The credit is either in the bank or payables account. The actual cost will be made up of all the indirect production costs – material, labour and expenses.

(2) The overheads that are absorbed into production (WIP) are recorded as a credit in the production overhead account. This is calculated as the budgeted OAR x actual activity.

(3) When the account is balanced at the end of the period and the balancing amount is required on the debit side of the account to equal the credit side we have an over-absorption of overheads. The overheads absorbed into production are greater than the actual cost of the overheads. This is recorded as a credit in the costing statement of profit or loss.

(4) When the account is balanced at the end of the period and the balancing amount is required on the credit side of the account to equal the debit side we have an under-absorption of overheads. The overheads absorbed into production are less than the actual cost of the overheads. This is recorded as a debit in the costing statement of profit or loss.

# Activity Based Costing

Activity based costing (ABC) is an alternative approach to product costing. It is a form of absorption costing, but, rather than absorbing overheads on a production volume basis it firstly allocates them to cost pools before absorbing them into units using cost drivers.

- A cost pool is an activity that consumes resources and for which overhead costs are identified and allocated. For each cost pool there should be a cost driver.

- A cost driver is a unit of activity that consumes resources. An alternative definition of a cost driver is the factor influencing the level of cost.

## Calculating the overhead recovery rate using ABC

There are five basic steps to calculating an activity based cost:

Step 1: Group production overheads into activities, according to how they are driven.

Step 2: Identify cost drivers for each activity, i.e. what causes these activity costs to be incurred.

Step 3: Calculate a cost driver rate for each activity.

Step 4: Absorb the activity costs into the product.

Step 5: Calculate the overhead cost per unit of product

# 7

# Short term decision making

- Assumptions of CVP analysis.
- Cost-Volume-Profit (CVP) analysis.
- Breakeven analysis.
- Profit volume (c/s) ratio.
- CVP charts.

## Assumptions of CVP analysis

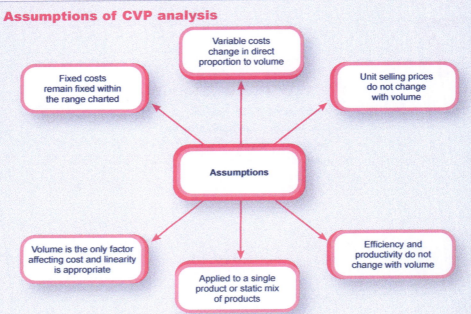

Variable costs change in direct proportion to volume

Fixed costs remain fixed within the range charted

Unit selling prices do not change with volume

**Assumptions**

Volume is the only factor affecting cost and linearity is appropriate

Applied to a single product or static mix of products

Efficiency and productivity do not change with volume

# Cost-Volume-Profit (CVP) analysis

## Definition

**Cost-Volume-Profit (CVP)** analysis: analysis of the effects of changes of volume on contribution and profit.

**Questions answered by CVP analysis:**

- How many units do we need to sell to make a profit?
- How much will profit fall by if the price is reduced by £1?
- What will happen to profits if we rent an extra factory and find we can only operate at half capacity?

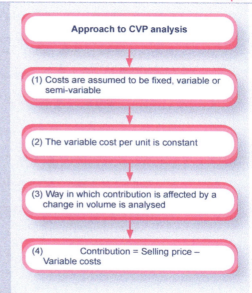

**Approach to CVP analysis**

(1) Costs are assumed to be fixed, variable or semi-variable

(2) The variable cost per unit is constant

(3) Way in which contribution is affected by a change in volume is analysed

(4) Contribution = Selling price – Variable costs

# Breakeven analysis

**Breakeven point**

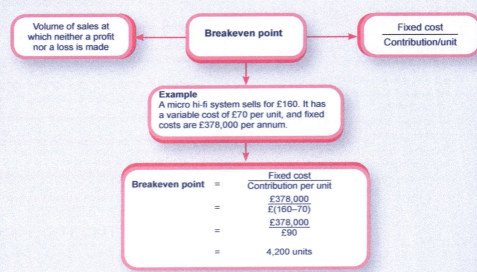

Volume of sales at which neither a profit nor a loss is made

**Breakeven point**

$$\frac{\text{Fixed cost}}{\text{Contribution/unit}}$$

**Example**
A micro hi-fi system sells for £160. It has a variable cost of £70 per unit, and fixed costs are £378,000 per annum.

Breakeven point $=$ $\dfrac{\text{Fixed cost}}{\text{Contribution per unit}}$

$$= \frac{£378,000}{£(160-70)}$$

$$= \frac{£378,000}{£90}$$

$$= 4,200 \text{ units}$$

## Margin of safety

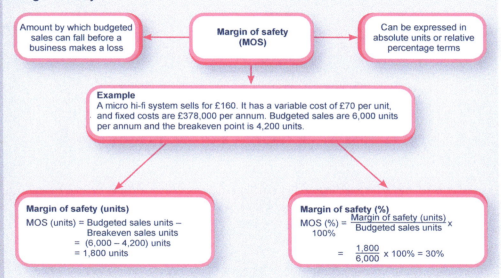

Amount by which budgeted sales can fall before a business makes a loss

**Margin of safety (MOS)**

Can be expressed in absolute units or relative percentage terms

**Example**
A micro hi-fi system sells for £160. It has a variable cost of £70 per unit, and fixed costs are £378,000 per annum. Budgeted sales are 6,000 units per annum and the breakeven point is 4,200 units.

**Margin of safety (units)**
MOS (units) = Budgeted sales units – Breakeven sales units
= (6,000 – 4,200) units
= 1,800 units

**Margin of safety (%)**
$$\text{MOS (\%)} = \frac{\text{Margin of safety (units)}}{\text{Budgeted sales units}} \times 100\%$$

$$= \frac{1,800}{6,000} \times 100\% = 30\%$$

## Target profit

| Sales volume at which a particular profit it made | ← | **Target profit** | → | $\dfrac{\text{Total fixed costs} + \text{required profit}}{\text{Contribution/unit}}$ |

**Example**
A micro hi-fi system sells for £160.
It has a variable cost of £70 per unit, and fixed costs are £378,000 per annum.
The required profit for the year is £200,070.

To achieve a profit of £200,070 we require a contribution of £578,070 (fixed costs + required profit).

Sales volume for target profit of £200,070 $= \dfrac{\text{Fixed costs} + \text{required profit}}{\text{Contribution/unit}}$

$$= \frac{£378,000 + £200,070}{£160 - £70}$$

$$= \frac{£578,070}{£90} = 6,423 \text{ units}$$

# Profit volume (c/s) ratio

A measure of the rate at which profit (or contribution) is generated with sales volume ◄— **PV ratio** —► $\text{P/V ratio} = \dfrac{\text{Contribution}}{\text{Selling price}}$

**Example**
A micro hi-fi system sells for £160 and has a variable cost of £70 per unit

$$
\begin{aligned}
\text{P/V ratio} &= \frac{\text{Contribution}}{\text{Selling price}} \\[6pt]
&= \frac{£160 - £70}{£160} \\[6pt]
&= \frac{£90}{£160} = 0.5625
\end{aligned}
$$

**The profit volume ratio is also known as the C/S (contribution/sales) ratio**

The profit volume ratio can be used in the BEP and target profit formulae instead of contribution per unit to calculate revenue amounts rather than units.

## CVP charts

**Breakeven chart showing fixed and variable cost lines**

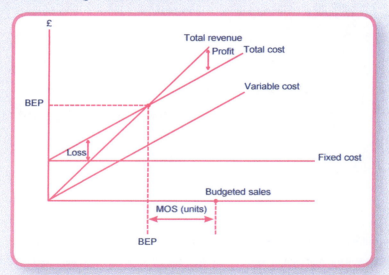

## Profit-volume (c/s) chart

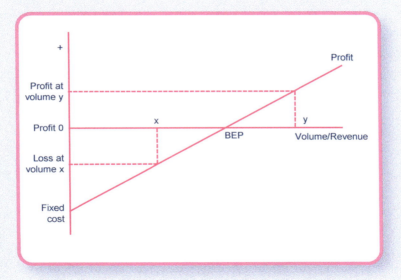

# 8

# Budgets and variance analysis

- Types of budgets.
- Variance analysis.
- Types of variances.

## Types of budgets

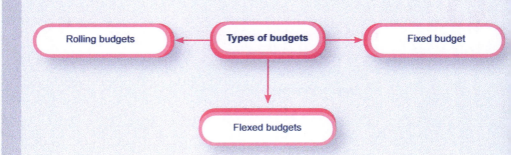

# Variance analysis

The aim is to be able to compare the costs and revenues of the activity that has actually been completed with what revenue and cost that level of activity should have produced. To be able to make this comparison a flexed budget needs to be produced.

## Flexed budgets

A flexed budget calculates the costs and revenues at certain levels of activity based on the budget costs.

To be able to produce a flexed budget a good knowledge of cost behaviours is required – see chapter 2.

## Overview of cost behaviours:

- Variable – increases in direct proportion with the level of activity and is constant per unit.
- Fixed – remains constant in total at all levels of activity.
- Stepped – remains constant in total to a certain level of activity and then the cost steps up to a new higher constant.
- Semi-variable – there is a fixed element to the cost and a variable element. These costs are separable using the high-low method.

### An example of a flexed budget

| Units sold and produced | Cost or revenue per unit | 1,200 | 1,800 | 2,500 |
|---|---|---|---|---|
| | £ | £ | £ | £ |
| Sales Revenue | 20 | 24,000 | 36,000 | 50,000 |
| Direct Materials | 2.50 | 3,000 | 4,500 | 6,250 |
| Direct Labour | 4.70 | 5,640 | 8,460 | 11,750 |
| Variable Overheads | 3.50 | 4,200 | 6,300 | 8,750 |
| Fixed cost | | 6,290 | 6,290 | 6,290 |
| Total profit | | 4,870 | 10,450 | 16,960 |
| Profit per unit (2 decimal places) | | 4.06 | 5.81 | 6.78 |

### Variance analysis

Once a flexed budget is produced to match the actual levels of sales and production the costs and revenues are compared.

A favourable variance occurs if the actual revenue received is greater than the flexed revenue or if the actual costs are less than the flexed costs.

An adverse variance occurs if the actual revenue is less than the flexed revenue or if the actual costs are greater than the flexed costs.

## An example of a variance statement

|  | Flexed Budget | Actual | Variance value | Favourable or Adverse | Percentage change % |
|---|---|---|---|---|---|
| Volume Sold | 1,370 | 1,370 |  |  |  |
|  | £ | £ | £ |  |  |
| Sales Revenue | 27,400 | 30,000 | 2,600 | F | 9.5 |
| Less costs: |  |  |  |  |  |
| Direct Materials | 3,425 | 3,875 | 450 | A | 13.1 |
| Direct Labour | 6,439 | 6,501 | 62 | A | 1.0 |
| Variable overheads | 4,795 | 4,975 | 180 | A | 3.8 |
| Fixed cost | 6,290 | 6,300 | 10 | A | 0.2 |
| Operating profit | 6,451 | 8,349 | 1,898 | F |  |

### Reconciliation of actual with budget

Once the variances have been calculated it is possible to reconcile the actual profit with the bugeted profit.

- An adverse variance will decrease the budgeted profit so this is subtracted from budgeted profit.

- A favourable variance will increase the budgeted profit so this is added to the budgeted profit.

# Types of variances

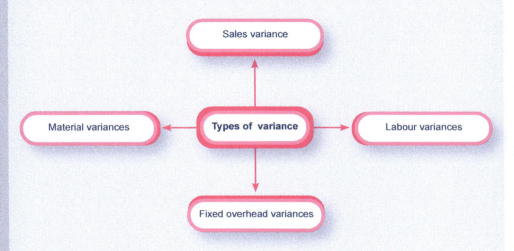

chapter

# 9

# Principles of cash budgeting

- Cash flow and profit.
- Forecasting cash flows.
- Cash budgets.
- Working capital cycle.
- Raising finance.
- Accounting software for cash flows.

# Cash flow and profit

Cash and profit are not the same thing. It is possible for a business to make a profit but to also run short of cash.

- Profit is a figure on the Statement of profit or loss.
- Cash is a current asset on the Statement of financial position.

**The difference between cash and profit**

- Revenue
- Costs
- Accruals
- Prepayments
- Depreciation
- Provision for doubtful debts
- Purchases of non-current assets
- Sale of non-current assets
- Financing transactions

# Forecasting cash flows

To be able to produce a cash budget the actual cash a business spends and receives during a time period needs to be calculated.

Information needed:

- Sales information
- Production information
- Accounting information
- Forecast information

# Cash budgets

A cash budget or cash flow forecast is an **estimate of all of the cash inflows and outflows for the period.**

Remember that a cash budget monitors cash – do not include any non-cash items i.e. depreciation.

# Working capital cycle

## Liquidity

Liquidity is the measure of surplus cash and near cash, over and above the level required to meet obligations.

Working with capital is the short-term net assets of the business made up of inventory, receivables, payables and cash.

## Calculating the working capital cycle

The working capital cycle can be calculated in days using the following formulae:

Trade receivable collection period (days) $= \dfrac{\text{trade receivables}}{\text{revenue}} \times 365$

Trade payable payment period (days) $= \dfrac{\text{trade payables}}{\text{cost of sales}} \times 365$

Inventory holding period (days) $= \dfrac{\text{inventories}}{\text{cost of sales}} \times 365$

The **Working capital cycle (days)** is calculated as:

**Inventory days + Receivable days − Payable days**

# Raising finance

At various stages in a business's life cycle the management may find that there is a need to raise additional finance. There are many reasons why a business may need to raise additional finance but the most common are:

- to fund working capital
- to increase working capital
- to reduce payables
- to purchase non-current assets
- to acquire another business.

# Accounting software for cash flows

### Automation and visualisation

When producing cash flow forecasts and budgets spreadsheets can be very useful. One of the most useful functions of a spreadsheet is being able to input formulae to enable calculation to happen automatically when data is input in specific cells. Most spreadsheet software also allows for graphs and charts to be produced, allowing users of the reports to visually see how the cash levels change over time.

# 10

# Spreadsheets for management accounts

- Spreadsheet basics.
- Sort and filter.
- Formulas and basic functions.
- Cell referencing.
- Conditional formatting.
- Subtotalling.
- Useful and logical functions.
- Formula auditing.
- Graphs and charts.
- Data Validation.
- Protecting your data.
- Pivot tables.

## Spreadsheet basics

### Formatting

Formatting is a process whereby you change the visual aspects of your worksheet.

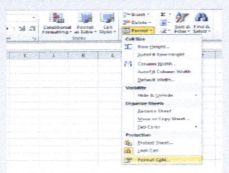

**Number** Changes number formats, for example the number of decimal places, currency type or percentages.

**Alignment** Allows adjustment of where data is shown within a cell for example left or right alignment, and merging cells together.

**Font** Appearance and size of text, along with special features like bold and underline.

**Border** Affects the cell itself, rather than the data within – place lines of varying size and colours around the cell.

**Fill** Colour the cell in various shades and patterns.

**Protection** Affects whether a cell can be edited.

To Exit the menu, click OK to accept any changes, or Cancel to reject them.

## Viewing formulas

Viewing formulas is very useful to be able to check what has been used and where. In the **Formulas** tab, select **Show Formulas**.

**Ctrl + `** [control and grave] will do the same as above.

## Sort and filter

Sometimes you will need to change the order of your data so that it is sorted according to your requirements. This can be performed quickly and easily, using the Sort function, located in both the **Home** tab and the **Data** tab.

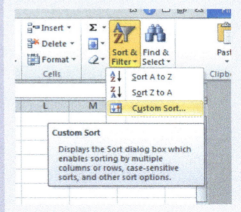

Sort A to Z and Z to A will sort data into either ascending order or descending order. This may not be what you need, so Custom Sort is usually what is required.

### Sorting by date

Choose custom list when sorting by month or days, and select the relevant list required. The data will then be sorted as required.

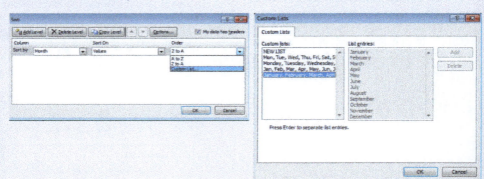

## Filtering data

Filtering data is a powerful way of quickly analysing large data sets to find the information you need.

To apply **AutoFilter**, select the data you wish to analyse, and click the Filter button.

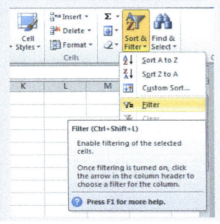

To remove a filter either click back in the filter and **Select All**, or within the **Sort & Filter** button, click the **Clear** option.

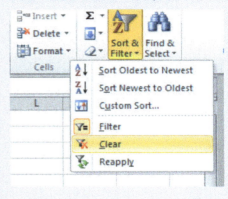

# Formulas and basic functions

Excel's primary purpose is to manipulate raw data through calculations and formulae. One of the main things you will use Excel for is simple calculations. The most basic calculations are the mathematical functions of addition +, subtraction -, multiplication * and divide /.

## Operators and order of preference

| Operator | Symbol | Order of Precedence |
|----------|--------|---------------------|
| Brackets | () | 1 |
| Multiplication | * | 2 |
| Division | / | 2 |
| Addition | + | 3 |
| Subtraction | - | 3 |

## Using functions

To enter a function into a cell, always start with an **EQUALS SIGN** first.

You then type the **NAME** of the function, followed by an **OPEN BRACKET** (.

The **ARGUMENTS** of the function are then required. These tell Excel exactly what to do, and depend on the function required. If more than one argument is needed, they must be separated by a **COMMA**.

The function is ended with a **CLOSE BRACKET** ).

## The Insert Function button

The **Insert Function** button $f_x$ located just above the column names:

Clicking this button brings up the **Insert Function** menu, which can help work out which function is required.

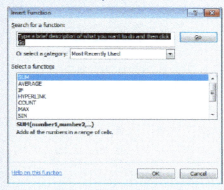

The most commonly used functions include:

=sum

=average

=max

=min

These can also be found by using the **Autosum** shortcut on the **Home** tab.

## Cell referencing

There are three types of cell referencing:

**Relative cell referencing**

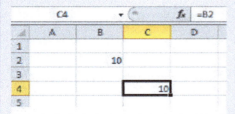

The formula in cell C4 is = **B2**. This means that when the value in cell B2 is changed, C4 will be updated to show this (C4 is **LINKED** to B2).

With relative referencing like this, if you **Copy** and **Paste** the formula in cell C4 into another cell, the reference to B2 will change. The way it works is as follows:

- If you copy the formula **UP**, the row number decreases.
- If you copy the formula **DOWN**, the row number increases.
- If you copy the formula **RIGHT**, the column letter increases.
- If you copy the formula **LEFT**, the column letter decreases.

If we copy the formula into cell D3:

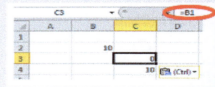

Here you can see the formula has been copied UP a row, so the row number in the reference has reduced by one. As there is no entry in cell B1, the result is shown as zero.

## Absolute cell referencing

This is used to ensure that a formula always looks at the content of a particular cell or range of cells. This is very useful for V and H Lookups and 'what-if' analysis when you are looking at particular scenarios.

To create an **Absolute** reference we use a $ sign before the letter and the number in the cell reference:

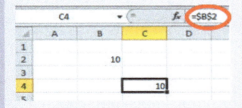

## Mixed cell referencing

This is a combination of both **Absolute** and **Relative** referencing.

We want to calculate basic pay:

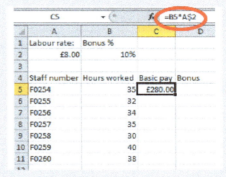

When the formula is copied down, the **$2** in the reference to cell A2 means that the row will remain fixed. You can copy the formula across, and the bonus is correctly calculated based on cell **B2** – because there is no $ before the A in the original formula, the column is not fixed.

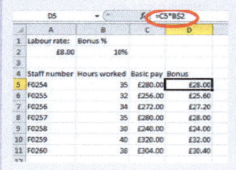

### Referencing other worksheets

It is very common that a calculation will need to refer to a cell on another worksheet within the same workbook. This works in the same way, but now instead of saying "Use the value in cell A1", we need to say "Use the

value in Cell A1 on Sheet 2" (for example). The format for this would be:

**='Sheet 2'!A1**

The 'A1' part of the formula is referring to cell A1 – to specify the sheet name, use the quote marks, followed by an exclamation mark.

Remember that when entering a formula, you can click on the cell you wish to use rather than typing its reference. This is true whether the cell is on the current worksheet or not.

# Conditional formatting

Conditional Formatting is where you can change the format of a cell based on certain conditions. For example you could want to colour a cell in red if its value is less than a certain number, or make the font bold if its value is equal to a number:

Clicking **New Rule** from the **Rules Manager** menu brings up the following options:

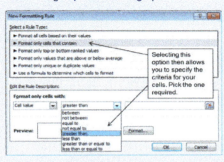

Set up the rule and the required formating and click ok to apply.

It is possible to have up to 64 conditional formatting rules for any cell. Extra rules are added in the same way as a new rule – select the cells required and create a new rule.

**Edit** rules from within the **Rules Manager** box:

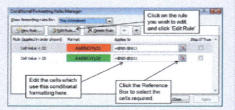

Use the **Rules Manager** to delete a rule in the same way. Alternatively, all rules can be deleted through the **Conditional Formatting** button in the **Home Menu**.

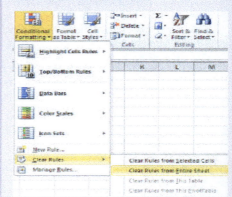

## Subtotalling

The Subtotal function is found in the Data tab, in the Outline menu.

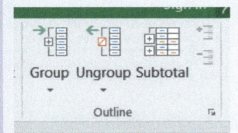

**Important note** – in order for a subtotal to work, the data MUST be sorted first, in the same order as the column(s) you wish to subtotal by.

### Grouping

Some extra buttons may appear on the left of the sheet– these allow you to quickly hide and show data. Clicking on the [–] boxes will hide the data and they become [+]. Clicking the [+] will unhide the data.

### Removing subtotals

Removing subtotals is done in a similar way to adding subtotals – select the data with the subtotals on, and click the **Subtotal** button.

Click the **Remove All** button the remove the subtotals.

### Multiple subtotals

Note: If you already have a subtotal in place, it will be overwritten as **Replace current subtotals** is selected.

# Useful and logical functions

## ROUND

Instead of changing the format, you may wish to instruct Excel to round the numbers to a certain number of decimal places – this is often useful when dealing with currency – round to 2 decimal places. To do this, use the **ROUND** function:

**=ROUND(number,num_digits)**

- 'number' and 'num_digits' are the ARGUMENTS.
- **number** is the number or cell reference which needs rounding.
- **num_digits** is the number of decimal places you wish to round to.

The ROUND function follows normal mathematical rounding rules – 0-4 are rounded down and 5-9 are rounded up.

Sometimes you will want to force a number to be rounded up or down, and ROUNDUP or ROUNDDOWN will do this.

## LOOKUPS

LOOKUPs can be used to interrogate large 'blocks' of data, and find the information required – linking the two together, so if the original is edited, the other spreadsheet will be too.

## VLOOKUP

VLOOKUP is used when the data is in columns.

**=VLOOKUP(lookup_value,table_array,col_index_num,[range_lookup])**

- **lookup_value** – this is the data item you are looking for.
- **table_array** – this is the range the data is in – i.e. where you are looking. The first column should contain the item being looked up and absolute

referencing needs to be added to ensure that Excel continues to look at the correct data if the vlookup is being used in more than one cell.

- **col_index_number** – this is the column number we want to use from the table_array.

- **[range lookup]** – this should either be TRUE or FALSE. The square brackets indicate that this is an optional argument. If you leave it out then Excel will assume its value is TRUE.

- FALSE means that an exact match to the lookup_value must be found – useful for looking up specific items in a list.

- TRUE means the nearest value to the lookup_value will be found – useful if there is a range of values that the lookup_value lies between.

**HLOOKUP** works in a very similar way to **VLOOKUP** but it is a horizontal lookup – the data will be in rows rather than columns. Excel will search along a row to find the value, and then return the value in the specified row of the table.

**Logical functions**

Logical functions give an answer of either **TRUE** or **FALSE**.

**IF**

IF functions can be used to give a response other than true or false

**IF**

IF is used to see a criteria has been met

=IF(logical_test,[value_if_true],[value_if_false])

- **Logical_test** – as above, a logical test is a test that will have the value TRUE or FALSE. What are we testing?

- **Value_if_true** – enter here what you would like to do if the test is true – this could be a calculation, some text or even another Excel function. What to do if the test is true.

- **Value_if_false** – enter here what to do if the test is false, in the same way. What to do if the test is false.

### AND and OR

AND and OR functions return true or false but can be combined with an IF functions to give a different response.

### AND

AND is used when you want to check more than one thing is true. As it is a logical function, the result of an AND function will be TRUE or FALSE.

=AND([logical1,[logical2], ...)

### OR

OR works in a similar way to AND, but this time we are checking is this true OR is this true OR is this true.

=OR(logical1,[logical2], ....)

### GOAL SEEK

Goal Seek can be found in the **Data** tab, in the **Forecast** section within the What-if Analysis menu.

**Goal Seek** is a tool used to find the right input for the value you want.

# Formula auditing

## Errors

| Error | Description |
|-------|-------------|
| #DIV/0! | This occurs if we have tried to divide by zero or a blank cell. |
| #N/A | This occurs if data is not available. It is common in LOOKUP functions. |
| #NAME? | This occurs if we use a name that Excel doesn't recognise. This is common in incorrectly spelled function names. |
| #NUM! | This occurs if you place an invalid argument in a function. |
| #REF! | This occurs if a formula uses an invalid cell reference. |
| #VALUE! | This occurs if we attempt to use an incorrect data type. |

The **Formula Auditing Toolbar** is a very useful tool for finding and controlling errors in spreadsheets – especially complex ones. It is found in the **Formulas** tab.

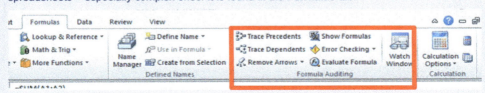

## Graphs and charts

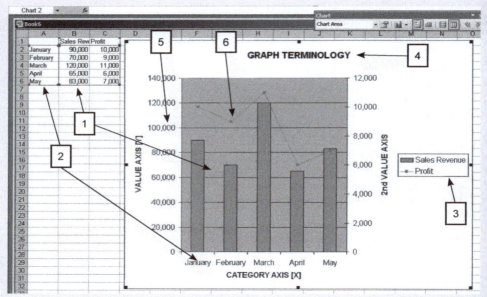

1.  **Data Series** – these are the numbers **[values]** from which Excel is creating the graph. These are plotted on the **Value or 'Y' axis.**

2.  **Category** – the information that identifies the data series. This is plotted along the **Category or 'X' axis**.

3.  **Legend** – this identifies the different data series.

4.  **Title** – gives meaning to the graph.

5.  **Scale** – both the 'X' and the 'Y' axis (if numerical) can have a scale. These identify the range of values in the data series.

6.  **Data Point** – this denotes the value of a particular data series. **Data Labels** can be placed next to data points to give greater meaning. Data Points have Data Markers. **Data Markers** are different shapes and colours for each data series.

## Design Tab

This is to do with the fundamental features of your chart – what sort of chart it is, the data used and where it is shown on your spreadsheet.

## Format Tab

This tab allows you to change the format of any aspect of your graph.

# Data Validation

Data validation allows a user to restrict what values can be entered into a cell. This can prevent incorrect data entry, or allow another user to select from a Dropdown list, making data entry easier.

To add data validation, select the cell(s) required, then in the **Data** tab, select **Data Validation**.

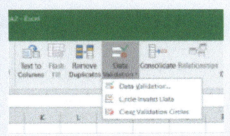

## Settings

This is where you define exactly how you would like to restrict your cell entry. The default is as shown above – **Allow: any value.** Selecting this dropdown box shows the options available.

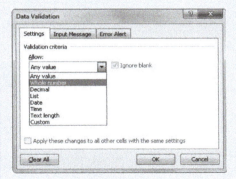

When an option is selected, more options become available. For example, whole number only allows whole numbers, but you can further restrict the range. As on many other options, you can restrict to certain ranges, or above or below other numbers (which can be based on cell values).

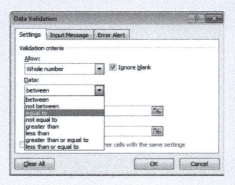

You can also restrict to a list of options. This is very useful when a cell should only contain certain entries.

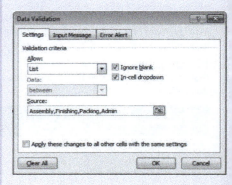

# Protecting your data

To prevent accidental/unauthorised changes to a worksheet, it must be protected. This is performed in the **Review** tab.

If you wish to protect one cell or a range of cells in a worksheet you can use **Allow Users to Edit Ranges** on the Review tab.

# Pivot tables

A Pivot Table is a tool used for turning tables of data into meaningful reports. The tool can be used to create reports from external sources, multiple-workbooks (another consolidation tool) and workbooks.

To create a pivot table, select the data (including headers) you wish to use, then in the Insert tab, select Pivot Table.

This opens the **PivotTable Wizard**.

You can also choose whether to create the table in a new worksheet or place it somewhere on your existing sheet.

This view allows you to build your report. The following terms are used:

- **Fields** – are the data headings used to make the report.
- **Report Filter** – this is the 'pages' of the report. For example we might have a page for every month, or every product.

- **Row Labels** – the rows of our report.
- **Column Labels** – the columns in our report.
- **Σ Values** – this is the 'data' in our report – the results we would like to show.

There is an alternative way to create a Pivot Table, which many people feel is more user-friendly. This may be displayed by default, but if your screen looks like the previous screenshot, you could try Classic View, in the Options tab, select Options.

In the Display tab select Classic Layout for a more user-friendly method of creating the Table.

The appearance of the table changes – as it says, you can now 'drag and drop' the field names onto the table if you prefer. There is no difference in terms of the final appearance, but many people prefer this method.

# Index

# Index

KAPLAN PUBLISHING

## S

## T

## U

## V

## W